IN THE DEEP BLUE SEA

Illustrated by Peter P. Plasencia

IN THE DEEP BLUE SEA

by

Elizabeth Morgan

Prentice-Hall, Inc., Englewood Cliffs, N. J.

to my mother and father

In the Deep Blue Sea, by Elizabeth Morgan

Library of Congress Catalog Card Number: 62-14740
Printed in the United States of America

45361-J (L)   45362-J (T)

Contents

I   *A traveling bottle*   7

II   *A bold journey*   12

III   *A very strange creature*   18

IV   *A "manfish"*   23

V   *Down we go*   29

VI   *The book of mud*   35

VII   *Treasure below*   41

VIII *Our fishy future*   51

IX   *Drifting pastures*   57

X   *A seahunt for facts*   64

CHAPTER I

A
traveling
bottle

Some day soon you may be standing on a beach and **PLOP!** A wave may drop a bottle at your feet.

Pick it up! Take a good look!

What's that inside? It looks like a rolled up card. Is it a message from a shipwrecked sailor? Or a map that will lead you to buried treasure?

Why don't you look closely and find out? If you are lucky, the card will say:

REWARD — REMOVE CARD FROM BOTTLE

Well, go ahead and take it out. It is a postcard, and the rest of its message is this:

PLEASE FILL IN INFORMATION
AS INDICATED, AND SEND BY MAIL

Where found (name of beach or place on shore, near what Coast Guard station, lighthouse, or other prominent reference point) . . . .
When found, date . . . .
Your Name (print) . . . .
Your Home Address (print) . . . .
Your return will assist the addressee in a study of coastal circulation.
Fifty cents plus location and date of release will be sent to finder on return of this card.

What is this all about? Should you fill in the card and mail it? Yes, you should. For when you do, you will be taking part in a very important scientific experiment. You will be helping the scientists who study the sea. These scientists are called *oceanographers* (*say: o-shun-OG-ra-fers*).

With the help of bottles like the one you may find, oceanographers are studying ocean currents. They stand on the deck of a ship and toss bottles into the water. Then surface currents carry the bottles far away.

Thousands of people like you have found these bottles and mailed in the cards. The cards go to the Woods Hole Oceanographic Institution in Massachusetts.

Oceanographer Dean F. Bumpus takes charge of them.

Each card tells him how far a bottle traveled from a ship. It also tells how many days the bottle drifted before it plopped at someone's feet.

Scientists at Woods Hole, and in the U. S. Fish and Wildlife Service, have some good reasons for learning these facts. Here is one good reason:

In the Gulf of Maine the cod and haddock have been disappearing. The eggs laid by these fish rise to the surface and drift in currents just as the bottles do. The scientists hope to follow the pattern of these currents, and find out what happens to some of the drifting eggs.

Have you gone swimming in the ocean? Then perhaps you have been caught in a current. It may have been an undercurrent made by the pull of the tides. This current rushes you along in the water. You can't swim against its strong force. Soon it drops you on the beach, far from the spot where you waded in.

Oceanographers are not sure why some currents act this way. Or why all currents are not alike. Some currents are warm and some are icy. Some rush along as fast as you can pedal your bike. Others poke along about as slow as a snail. Some currents run at the bottom of the sea. Others, such as the Gulf Stream, form great rushing rivers at the surface.

All of these currents make the ocean something like a giant mixing bowl. Food and oxygen are carried to fish living near the bottom of the sea. And food from the bottom is brought to the top.

The restless sea creates a problem for our country. For a long time scientists did not know that currents flowed in deep water. The deep, deep ocean seemed a good, quiet place to dump radioactive waste.

But currents might spread this radioactive waste. Fish might pick it up and pass it on to us when we eat them. Before we dump our radioactive waste into the deep blue sea, our scientists must learn more about currents.

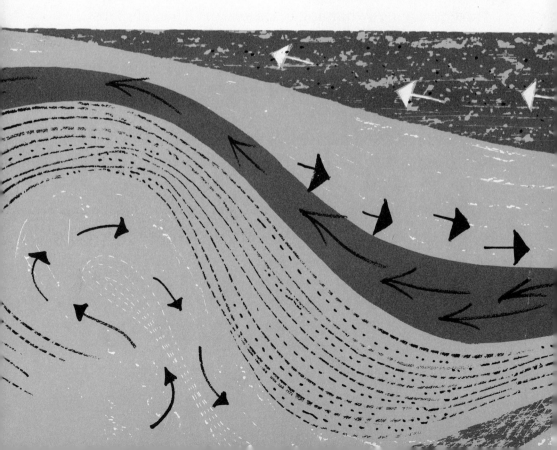

Our scientists, in fact, have a whole oceanful of facts to learn. Facts about fish, and buried treasures, and hidden mountains. In the past few years, scientists have been paying much more attention to the mysteries of outer space than they have to the sea.

The ocean is our "Inner Space," and it is much closer to us than the faraway moon and stars. It takes up two thirds of the surface of our own planet.

Why have we been slow about looking into this great world of water? Could it be that man was once afraid even to sail across the surface of the ocean? Let's go back into history and find out why.

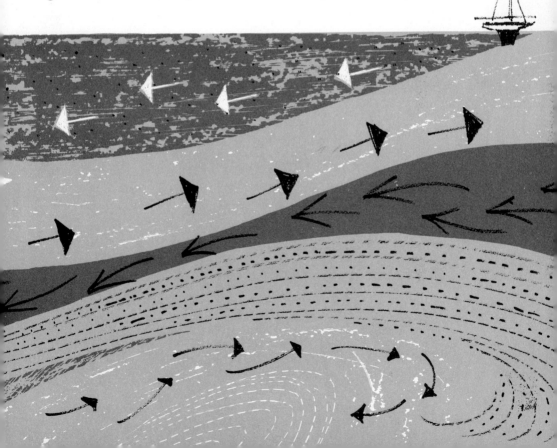

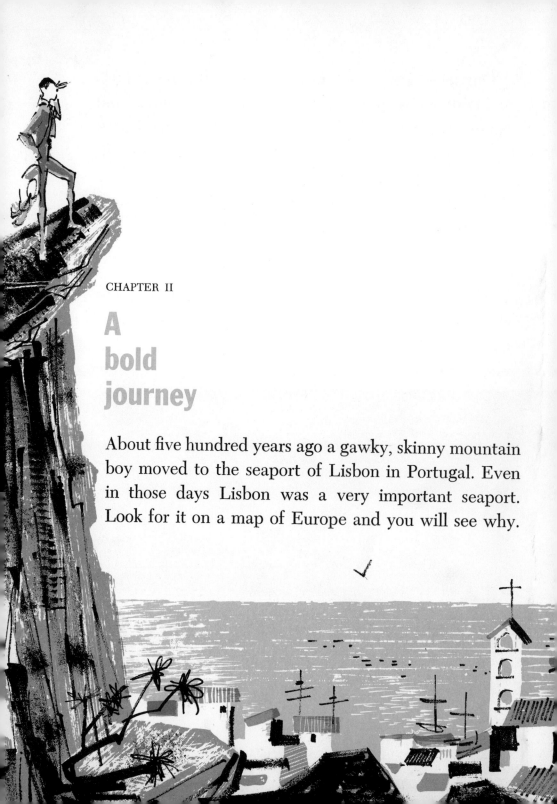

CHAPTER II

A bold journey

About five hundred years ago a gawky, skinny mountain boy moved to the seaport of Lisbon in Portugal. Even in those days Lisbon was a very important seaport. Look for it on a map of Europe and you will see why.

The boy's name was Ferdinand *Magellan* (*say: mah-JELL-an*). One warm, sunny day he strolled along the waterfront. For the first time in his life he looked out at the sea. The great rolling waves made his heart beat very fast. And he began to wonder.

What *other* shores did this mighty ocean touch? What strange people could live on those shores? Was there gold in the lands across the sea? Or were there no lands? Was the ocean just an endless waste of rolling water?

While he was growing up Ferdinand tried to learn all he could about the sea. But there was not much to learn.

Men, in those days, knew very little about the world we live in. Most men were afraid to sail more than a few miles from shore. They only went out to fish, or to trade at nearby seaports.

They believed some old and frightening stories about the sea. The stories had been passed down from father to son for many centuries. Here are some of them:

Around the coast of Africa, the sea was boiling hot. If a ship sailed to the south, it would be lost in darkness—forever.

Sea monsters lived in deep water. They waited to swallow up a ship and all of the men on it.

The world was flat. If a ship sailed over the horizon, it would drop off the edge of the world.

This last story was the worst. Men might take their chances with monsters, darkness, and a boiling sea. But they did not want to fall off the earth. So, year after year, and century after century, men did not do much exploring.

Magellan grew up to be as strong as steel. He would not let the old sea stories stop him. Explorers such as Columbus had found new lands. Magellan wanted to go even farther than they had.

In 1519 Magellan left a seaport in Spain, not too far from Lisbon, with five tiny ships. His little fleet sailed south across the Atlantic Ocean. The ships were old and frail, and they leaked when a storm blew up.

As the man of steel pushed across the unknown sea, his crewmen turned against him. They wanted to go home. The old sea stories scared them, and they were hungry and cold. But Magellan forced them on.

Around South America he sailed, and into the deep blue Pacific. One by one the ships were wrecked. The little fleet grew smaller.

The number of men grew smaller, too. They starved or froze or died from diseases. Magellan, himself, was killed in a fight with natives in what is now called the Philippine Islands.

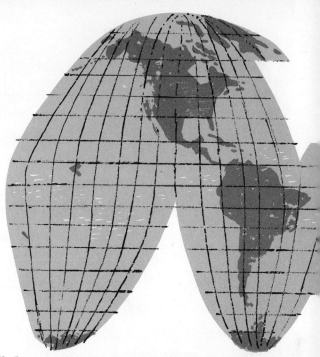

The World Ocean

But no one fell off the earth. No one was swallowed up by sea monsters. There was no eternal darkness or boiling sea.

Only one ship of Magellan's fleet made it across the Indian Ocean, and sailed up the west coast of Africa. In 1522, a handful of scraggly sailors steered the rickety ship, the *Victoria*, back to its starting point in Spain.

If you look at the map, you will see where Magellan sailed and where he died.

Magellan's voyage was a great triumph, because a new "path" was made across the sea. Other ships could follow the route that Magellan found. He was a great navigator.

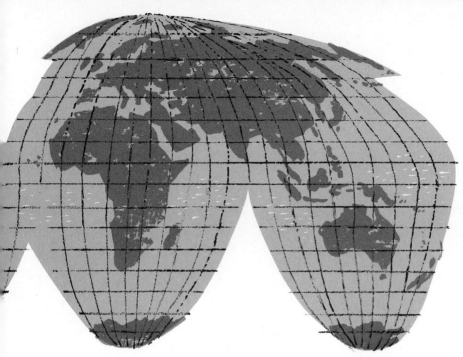

Other brave men took up where Magellan left off. In time, they found that the five great oceans are joined together. These are the Atlantic, Pacific, Indian, Arctic and the Antarctic. Together, they make one mighty ocean. Oceanographers call this *The World Ocean.*

Since Magellan's day, we have only skimmed over the surface of The World Ocean. It has taken us nearly five centuries to get really curious about the deeps—the watery world below.

But one thing about the deeps of the ocean has puzzled man all these centuries: Even if sea monsters *don't* live in the sea, what strange creatures *do?*

You shall soon find out!

CHAPTER III

A very strange creature

The deep blue sea is full of strange animals. Some are so tiny that you can't see them. Some are so big that you hope they can't see you. Sea creatures come in all sizes between the tiny ones and the giants.

They also come in all shapes. They are fat or thin and square or round. They can have big heads or pin heads and long or short tails. Sometimes you can't make heads or tails out of creatures in the sea.

As you know, many sea creatures are good to eat. Man has known this for a long time.

Thousands of years ago, our ancestors hunted fish in the sea, just as they hunted animals in the woods. They

18

waded out into shallow water and caught fish with their bare hands. Or stabbed them with sharp spears. Or shot them with bows and arrows.

The ancient Egyptians knew how to use nets to catch fish. And they knew how to sail boats. They caught fish in the Mediterranean, in the Red Sea, and in the Nile River.

Sea creatures meant so much to the Egyptians that their artists painted pictures of fish and squid. And they made beautiful toy fish out of colored glass.

The Egyptians caught many kinds of sea creatures. They were used to seeing all sizes and shapes. But there is one animal in the sea that they were not used to. This fish would have frightened them, because it is a *very* strange creature.

Even in our modern age, as short a time ago as 1938, this creature frightened some fishermen. Here is perhaps the strangest fish tale of all time:

Some fishermen were dropping nets into the Indian Ocean, near the east coast of South Africa. They hauled up the nets and dumped a catch of sharks and fish on the deck of their boat.

A scaly, steely-blue creature caught their eye. No one had ever seen anything like it. The creature was five feet long—probably longer than you are tall. It had a big mouthful of razor-sharp teeth and a nasty disposition. When the captain of the fishing boat leaned close to this beast, its teeth snapped fiercely at his hand.

When the boat got back to port, the fishermen dumped the rugged fish on the dock. It weighed 127 pounds—about as heavy as a woman of average size.

The fishermen showed the big creature to Miss M. Courtenay-Latimer. She was in charge of a local museum. Miss Latimer realized that this fish was a strange and special fish. She made a sketch and mailed it to Dr. J. L. B. Smith.

Smith was a professor of chemistry at a university in South Africa. But he also was an expert on fish, an *ichthyologist* (*say: ick-thih-AHL-o-jist*).

When Smith looked at the sketch, he could not believe his eyes. And yet, he was *sure* that he was staring at a sketch of a *coelacanth* (*say: SEE-la-kanth*).

How could this be? Scientists thought that the coelacanth had disappeared from the earth about seventy million years ago.

But there was the weird creature lying on a deck in South Africa: breathing, snapping, and waving its fins. It was just as alive as you are.

Scientific circles stirred with excitement. Even if a dinosaur had tramped along a city street, there would scarcely have been more excitement.

Scientists had seen many fossils of coelacanths. Imprints of their bodies had been preserved in ancient rocks. Somehow, this kind of creature had survived four

hundred million years of violent change on our earth. But the creature had not changed very much. The modern coelacanth looks much like its rock-bound, fossil ancestors.

A few other animals that survived almost unchanged from ancient times had been hauled out of the sea. And scientists thought more of these creatures might be hidden under water. But how could men look for these creatures? Men could not dive very deep, or stay long under the sea.

Just about this time, a Frenchman was getting ready to show the scientists how. Let's see how Capt. Jacques-Ives *Cousteau* (*say: koo-STOW*) turned himself into a "manfish."

CHAPTER IV

A
manfish

In 1936 Jacques Cousteau was a gunner in the French Navy. When he was not on regular duty, he liked to go skin diving in the clear, warm waters of the Mediterranean. He wore a glass mask on his face and rubber fins on his feet. In fact, he looked like a big, peculiar, one-eyed fish. (You would, too, if you went skin diving).

Cousteau almost *felt* like a fish. He could dart in and out of a school of sea creatures and tumble over and over just for fun.

But one thing kept reminding him that he was a man —he had to come up for air. Even when he took a great gulp of air before diving, he could stay underwater only a few minutes.

This really bothered Cousteau. There was a whole world to explore under the sea. How could he peek under rocks and poke into caves, if he had to come up for air all the time?

Something else bothered Cousteau. He could not dive very deep. Even the best skin divers in France could only dive down about sixty feet. And many exciting sights lay farther down.

Cousteau knew that some men had gone deeper. For thousands of years men had dived for pearls, sponges, shells, and the treasure of sunken ships. A few divers had taken one gulp of air and dived two hundred feet!

But this diving was very dangerous. Some men, helmet divers, were doing it a safer way. They wore heavy steel helmets over their heads and worked on the wrecks of ships, several hundred feet down in the ocean. They got air through a rubber hose which was hooked from their helmets to air pumps at the water's surface.

But helmet divers were not free to move around underwater. They were like horses tied to a tree. How could Cousteau tie himself to a boat and still explore the sea? He couldn't, of course. Somehow, he had to carry air with him.

But how? Cousteau and an engineer, Emile *Gagnan* (*say: GAN-yan*), found an answer. They invented the *aqualung*—small tanks of air hooked to a special valve, with a rubber tube to breathe through.

In 1943, Cousteau strapped the first aqualung on his back and dived into the Mediterranean. This time he did not have to come up after a few minutes for air. He stayed under and breathed almost as well as a man walking on dry land. And yet he could swim as freely as a fish.

Jacques Cousteau had turned into a "manfish."

Other skin divers — oceanographers, too — became "menfish." They could stay underwater for about two hours. And now they could dive two or three times deeper than they could without aqualungs. Menfish all over the world explored the strange and beautiful sea.

To a manfish, a coral reef is a wonderland of beauty. It is touched with rainbow colors—reds, yellows, blues, and greens. Thousands of gorgeous fish live in a reef like nobles in a great castle.

A reef is as strong as a rock and often as big as an island. But it is built by soft, tiny animals. How can this be?

Well, each coral animal has a skeleton made of limestone. New animals branch out from old ones. Their skeletons build up and up, one on top of another. Long after the soft animals die, their skeletons stay piled up together.

Some sights around a reef are not beautiful at all. They are downright ugly—and dangerous. Let's see what happened one sunny and peaceful day in the *Bahamas* (*say: Ba-HAH-mas*). You can find these islands on the map.

A diver was watching pretty little fish scamper in and out of a reef. Suddenly, he saw a dark, streamlined shape slicing through the water toward him. It was a shark.

The gray beast swam close, and quickly began to circle around the diver. The diver turned warily as it circled. He hoped to watch the shark's head and dodge quickly if it lunged at him.

Around and around they turned. The manfish kept a steady eye on the shark's snout, watching for its ugly mouth to open. The shark's eye flicked back and forth, looking the manfish over.

Soon, the whirling diver grew dizzy. He had to get off this deadly merry-go-round. But if he moved suddenly, the shark might bite. What could he do?

The diver took a chance and lunged at the shark. The shark darted away. The diver darted for his boat and escaped.

Divers may lunge at sharks and scare them away. But they try not to get near a *moray* eel (*say: MO-ray*). The ill-tempered moray tucks its snake-like body into a hole in a reef or a rock.

If a manfish happens to disturb it, the eel's needle-sharp teeth will snap at him with lightning speed. If a moray *really* gets disturbed, it will unwind from its hole and chase a diver clear around a reef.

What if *you* decide to strap on an aqualung and turn into a manfish some day? You will see this beautiful and dangerous world for yourself. You may want to go even deeper in the ocean than an aqualung will let you.

Adventuring scientists like Cousteau have found ways to go deeper. Let's see how men have dived thousands of feet down—deep into the gloom of the unknown sea.

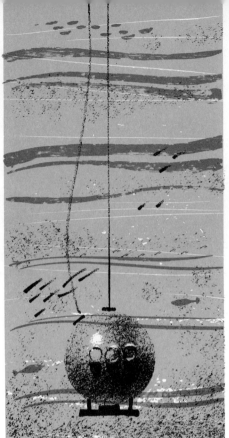

CHAPTER V

Down
we
go

Back in 1934, Dr. William Beebe and Otis Barton squeezed inside a hollow steel ball and plopped into the Atlantic Ocean. The ball dangled at the end of a steel cable which unwound slowly from the deck of a boat. The men called the ball a *bathysphere* (*say: BATH-i-sfeer*).

It was an odd looking ball. Barton himself said the bathysphere looked like a puffed up and "slightly cock-eyed bullfrog." Its portholes bulged like a frog's eyes.

The bathysphere was only four and a half feet wide. Why did two grown men get cramped into this contraption? Well, they wanted to find out what was going on deep in the sea.

The ball's steel walls were an inch and a half thick. The men needed this strong steel to protect them. Without it, water pressure would have crushed their bodies.

Pressure builds up as the ocean gets deep. Half a mile down, the pressure is more than a hundred times as great as it is at the ocean's surface. In the bathysphere, Beebe and Barton dived safely a half mile into the sea. This was much deeper than men had ever gone before.

The sea was as black as pitch, for sunlight does not reach this far. Was there, after all, anything to find in this lonely and dismal world?

Beebe soon found out. As he peered out through a porthole, and his eyes got used to the gloom, he saw a pair of shiny, frightful eyes peering back at him. They were the savage eyes of a giant squid.

Then a big red shrimp swam by, and flashed a brilliant red light. It made Beebe blink. Soon he saw that the whole black sea flashed with tiny lights, lights made by fish with special organs in their bodies. The creatures were lit up like fireworks on the Fourth of July.

For centuries men had believed that animals could not live in the deep sea. Beebe and Barton made several dives, and the teeming life they saw ended this belief forever. Scientists began to realize how little they knew about the depths of the ocean.

How could they learn more? The sea was much, much deeper than the bathysphere could go.

A Swiss explorer, Auguste *Piccard* (*say: pee-KAR*), solved the problem. He built a contraption which can dive to the bottom of the ocean. He called it a *bathyscaph* (*say: BATH-i-skaf*).

Two men fit into a steel ball which looks a lot like the old bathysphere. The ball is tucked under a long, cigar-shaped float. The bathyscaph really looks like a whale with a few extra bumps.

In 1960, Jacques Piccard, the son of Auguste, and Lieut. Don Walsh of the United States Navy dived seven miles down—to the deepest spot in the ocean. They touched the bottom of a giant trench in the Pacific. It is deep enough there to swallow up the tallest mountain on land.

Would you like to make a dive to this spot? Why don't you? You will be one of few humans who ever have.

Wriggle into the steel ball and shut the hatch. **CLANG!** Test the controls. **CLICK! SWITCH! WHIR!**

Now begin your dive—about as fast as an elevator falls.
SWISH!

Slowly, the sunlight fades away. At a thousand feet, only a pale glow filters through the water. Switch on the bathyscaph's powerful headlights. You will see snow streaming past the windows.

Wait a minute! It can't be snow. Look again! What you see are tiny, tiny creatures and specks of dust. Beams from the headlights make them look white.

Now, between two and three miles down, you enter the deepest part of the sea—the dark and silent *abyss* (*say: a-BISS*). A clammy chill creeps into your steel cabin, and you begin to shiver. Here you can see the weirdest creatures in the sea:

Fish with flabby, ghostly bodies. Fish with tiny "fishing poles" sticking out of their heads. Fish with light

organs like light bulbs in their mouths. Fish with light organs like miners' lamps above their eyes. Fish with no eyes at all.

Now slow the bathyscaph down. You are almost seven miles down. You don't want to crash into the bottom and get stuck there forever, do you? Slowly, slowly, ever so gently—**THUMP!** Now you are the deepest human in the whole world!

Look around. What do you see? A flat, clear bottom and few signs of life. A few tracks that worms have made. But what's that over there? It looks like a plain, ordinary flounder.

How can this be? Scientists thought bony fish like this would be crushed under such great water pressure. But Piccard and Walsh saw a flounder-like fish on their dive. Their discovery showed that a bony form of life *can* live in the deepest ocean.

What other familiar fish might be found down here? No one knows. This is a problem for other explorers, not for you. It's time for you to go home—up to the friendly world of sunlight and fresh air.

And when you get there, you will find out that there are other ways to explore the deep ocean. You won't even have to dive in.

The book of mud

On a starlit night a few years ago, a yellow metal monster clanked up a sandy beach. It had risen out of the Pacific Ocean near *La Jolla*, California (*say: La-HOY-a*).

The monster crawled along slowly on tank-like treads, and it shed an eerie green light. One giant, metal claw waved in the night, almost as if it were alive. The claw was about five times as long as a grownup's arm.

35

Had a visitor from outer space finally landed on earth? Or had a strange creature climbed up from the bottom of the sea? No. Nothing frightening like this had happened.

The monster was really a machine built by Dr. Victor Anderson, an oceanographer at the Scripps Institute of Oceanography in La Jolla.

Dr. Anderson calls his machine "The Beast." He controls the creature from shore and sends it clanking into the sea. "The Beast" is able to crawl along the ocean bottom into water four miles deep. This is a little more than half as deep as you dived in the bathyscaph.

The monster's claw picks up clumps of mud and rocks from the bottom of the sea. When "The Beast" clanks back to shore, Dr. Anderson takes the clumps to his laboratory. There, some scientists pick the clumps apart and look at the pieces under a microscope. And they make special chemical tests.

It may seem a little silly for grown men to spend their time studying mud and rocks. But scientists have good reasons. They know that important secrets about the earth are hidden in mud and rocks. What could these secrets be? Well, read this tale of ancient history and you will see.

The earth was formed about five billion years ago, and its early life was stormy and restless. Great howling winds whooshed the dust off mountaintops. Raging volcanoes hurled out ashes and rocks. Thundering floods swept up silt and rocks. Tons of the dust, ashes, silt, and rocks were dumped into the ocean.

As ages passed and the earth warmed, icy glaciers crunched to the sea. The glaciers picked up dirt and rocks along the way. This stuff, too, was dumped in the sea. And through the ages, tiny bits of shells, plants, and animals have drifted slowly down to the ocean floor.

Now, after all these ages, there must be a million billion TRILLION little particles piled up on the bottom of the sea. This great heap is what we have been calling mud. Scientists would rather call the particles *sediments* (*say: SED-i-ments*). Some rocks are called sedimentary rocks.

So, if we figure out where the sediments came from, we can tell what was going on back in the ages of the earth's great upheavals. And we can tell when the upheavals happened, for the sediments have settled down in a certain way. They have made a clear record of mountain building, ice forming, volcanoes, earthquakes, and floods.

In other words, the earth's history is written in the sediments—a giant book of mud.

A great deal of this book is a deep dark secret, like a book in some unknown tongue. Bit by bit, the scientists must figure out what the particles mean. This is why they bring up clumps of sediments from the ocean floor.

Many sediments lie too deep and far away for "The Beast" to reach. So, scientists themselves go "digging" in the sea. They dig deep into the mud which is piled up for hundreds of feet on the ocean floor. How do they get to these deep sediments?

Well, the first thing they do is climb aboard a ship and set out to sea. When they find a spot where they want to "dig," they stand on deck and hook ropes to *coring tubes*. These tubes are long, hollow pipes.

The scientists heave the tubes over the side. The tubes plunk into the water and soon plunge deep into the sediments. They cut out a long column of mud. Then the scientists haul up the tubes. The mud they want to study is stuck inside the tubes.

A few scientists, directed by Willard Bascom, are even drilling into the hard crust which lies beneath the thick sediments.

Why? What are the scientists trying to get at, so deep down under tons and tons of mud and water?

Rocks. If they can bring up rocks from the earth's insides, they can find answers to questions like these: What is the earth made of? How was it formed those five billion years ago?

Bascom's men plan to drill holes deeper and deeper—until they drill a hole six miles down. They will call this hole the *Mohole*. *Project Mohole* is being sponsored by the National Academy of Sciences and the National Science Foundation.

Whenever the hole gets dug, newspapers and television will tell you about it. For the Mohole will reach deeper into the earth than man has ever reached before!

The rocks brought up from this deep hole will be a great treasure from the earth's insides. Just as sediments are treasures from the ocean floor. There are a great many other ocean treasures, too. Let's take a look at how some of them got into the sea, and how we get them out.

CHAPTER VII

Treasure below

At the eastern end of the Mediterranean, nearly two thousand years ago, a king built a proud and beautiful city. He named the city Caesarea (*say: see-suh-REE-uh*). The king's workmen set massive blocks of stone out in the sea and made an encircling wall. The wall formed a sheltering harbor for little cargo ships that sailed from across the sea.

41

Giant statues of marble and red granite stood high above the harbor's entrance. Famous men, such as St. Peter and St. Paul, must have looked up at these statues on their journeys from old Palestine.

But winds and waves, earthquakes and wars, slowly killed the brilliant city. The handsome statues and the great harbor wall toppled into the sea. And today, twenty feet of water cover much of the city's crumbled remains.

In 1961, Edwin Link took a crew of aqualung divers on a treasure hunt to this dead city. The divers found parts of the great statues lying in the clear, green water. Pots and vases which told of life in Caesarea were dug out of thick mud on the bottom.

To the divers these treasures were important, for this was a new kind of treasure hunt—a seahunt into man's history. Some day soon, the divers hope to take another look at what is left of Caesarea.

The Mediterranean is a good place to look for historical treasures, for the ancient world grew up around this sea. Frail little ships sailed to and fro, carrying art treasures and cargoes of household goods. The unlucky little ships often sank in a storm and littered the bottom with their cargoes. Modern divers have made a sport and a science out of hunts for these remains.

In the Aegean Sea ancient galleys with oars and sails used to pick their way through the rocky islands. On one rocky reef, only six feet deep, the ships often ripped their hulls and sank.

Not long ago Peter Throckmorton and his diving crew discovered a ship that had been wrecked in 1400 B.C. It is the oldest shipwreck ever found! The divers brought up some age-old relics: heavy hunks of copper, bronze picks, axes and chisels, clay pots, and jugs that once held oil or wine.

Treasures like these won't make you rich. But the hunt for them is exciting. And the relics may tell us more than we now know about our ancient history. But even a history hunter may hope to stumble across a treasure of real gold and jewels.

When Spaniards settled in the New World, they stole great treasures from the South American Indians. They loaded millions of dollars in gold, silver, and jewels into clumsy ships and sent them off to Spain. Many of these creaking galleons broke up on the coral reefs of the Caribbean. And the fabulous treasures were lost.

Some men went to sea and found part of this great wealth. But today much of the old Spanish loot lies untouched on the bottom of the sea. On a reef near the Florida Keys rests sixty-eight million dollars worth. And there the gold waits for a bold diver to bring it up. Perhaps, some day, that diver will be *you!*

Meanwhile, some men are finding more practical treasures. Minerals such as uranium, manganese, copper, silver, and gold are dissolved in the ocean water. About sixty valuable minerals slosh around in the sea, and oceanographers would like to take them out.

Great amounts of bromine and magnesium are taken out of sea water. Bromine goes into gasoline to run our cars and trucks. Magnesium, a metal of very light weight, is used in building airplanes.

Perhaps the richest supply of minerals is found on the ocean floor. Here there are countless clumps of nodules (*say: NOD-yools*) which are made of manganese, cobalt, copper, nickel, and iron. They look like big potatoes.

Clusters of these nodules are scattered over great areas of the ocean floor—in the Atlantic, the Pacific, and the Indian oceans. How did the nodules get down there? And how are we going to get them up? No one knows either answer. But Dr. John Mero has a good idea for picking them up:

Why not build a giant vacuum cleaner, and suck the clumps up into the hold of a ship?

Oil, one of the sea's greatest treasures, is pumped out of the ocean floor. Vast deposits of this "black gold" are found in the shallow bottoms around our continents. As far as we know, these deposits make up one-third of all the oil left on earth.

Since the 1930's, our oil companies have drilled offshore—near the coast of California and in the Gulf of Mexico. Here is how they do it:

A barge tows a big steel platform out to the place

where the well will be drilled. Long steel legs slide
down from the platform and sink into the ocean floor.
They hold the platform steady while the bit of the drill

whirls around and around. The bit bites slowly through the mud and rocks of the shallow bottom of the sea. If the bit strikes oil, men on the drilling rig can set up a pump. Or they can put a strong cap on the well, and pump the oil out later.

Well, now that you have found some treasures in the sea, which one is the most important? You probably can't guess, because the greatest treasure is—water!

The world is running short of fresh water. Each year, we need more to drink, to water our crops, and to run our industries. Ninety-nine per cent of all the water in the world sloshes around in the great ocean basins. And we can't use a drop unless we take out the salt.

Salt water would make us sick and kill our crops. And it would really gum up the works in industry. Can we turn the ocean into fresh water?

Yes, we can. But it is going to cost us a lot of money. Our government has built a converting plant at Freeport, Texas. Each day this plant makes a million gallons of fresh water from the sea.

So far, it seems to be working out well. The plant can turn out a thousand gallons of fresh water for a dollar. This is just half the cost of water which is desalted at plants in the rest of the world.

Our scientists hope to cut the cost down to fifty cents. The government is going to give them plenty of chances to try. For there are plans to build four more plants around the country.

What *is* the world's water future? Well, *we* probably will always get enough fresh water. And if our plans work out, perhaps we can show other countries how to desalt water cheaply. But right now, people in sixty countries do not get enough.

And their future is faced with another shortage, too. Soon they may not get enough fish to eat. And we may not get enough either. Let's see what the world's fish future is going to be.

CHAPTER VIII

Our fishy future

Picture yourself playing on a beautiful red beach in Nova Scotia (*say: NO-va SKO-sha*). You can find this place on the map of Canada.

You are skipping across this delightful beach which stretches far and wide along the Bay of Fundy. Suddenly, you stop in your tracks. Something very peculiar is going on. What do you see?

Well, men are standing on step ladders in the middle of the beach, and the ladders are propped against a huge net. The net swings high from strong poles which are jammed deep down in the sand. The net stretches a thousand feet across the beach.

51

What are the men doing on those ladders?

They are picking fish! Shad and salmon hang from the net like peaches hang from a tree.

How did the fish get up there?

Well, twice each day, a rumbling and hissing tide sweeps in and buries the beach under tons of water. The net is completely covered. The tide that dashes up this beach is the greatest in all the world.

Thousands of fish are swept up in the force of the rushing sea. When the tide rushes out again, the fish are caught high and dry in the net. Then the men climb up on their ladders and pluck the fish from the net as fast as they can. When the tide gets ready to race in again, later in the day, the fish pickers pack up and run for their lives!

This is an exciting way to go fishing. But the men don't catch many fish, because this method is very crude. Wherever crude ways of fishing are used, the fish catch is less than it should be.

If we don't start catching more fish, some day we may really go hungry for these creatures. Each year the world's population grows a little. The extra people want to eat fish, too.

There are plenty of fish in the sea. But we can't always catch them when we want to. Sometimes the creatures are hard to find, and sometimes they dart away before fishermen can haul them up.

Even now fishermen in the United States don't haul up enough fish to feed us. We have to buy seafood from other countries. As the years go by, we will need more and more.

How *are* we going to get enough fish in the future? Well, for one thing, more fishermen can use the new ways to hunt for fish. Ways like these:

An airplane zooms low over Maine's coastal waters, while fishermen stand by on their boats. The airplane's pilot peers into the sea, looking for a school of silvery herring. When he finds the little fish, he talks on his radio and tells the men where they are.

Fishermen drag a tiny instrument through the waters of Europe's North Sea. It counts the number of drifting *plankton* (*say: PLANK-tun*). Big fish feed on these tiny plants and animals. So, the fishermen follow where the counts of the instrument lead them. And they find good fishing—right in the middle of a plankton patch.

In the Caspian Sea, some fishermen don't hunt for fish. They hang bright lights down in the water. When the fish swim up to the lights, they get sucked up into the boats with suction pumps.

In some places, we have "planted" fish so fishermen can catch them. We shifted shad, striped bass, and the soft clam from the Atlantic to the Pacific Ocean. We picked up our Chinook salmon and planted it in the waters around New Zealand.

But, most of our tries at transplanting fish have failed. The fish often die in strange waters, and we don't know exactly why. We still have a great deal to learn about how creatures live in the sea.

The first few weeks of a young fish's life are very dangerous weeks. Only one fish in a hundred small fish lives through them. If only we could find a way to save all the other tiny ones from death. Think how many big fish we could eat some day!

In the deep and dangerous sea every fish has its own

deadly enemies. Little herring are gobbled up by tuna, and tuna are munched on by great killer whales.

Suppose we raised fish in the shallow ponds and marshes sheltered by our seacoasts. We could protect them from their enemies. They could grow up fat and healthy. In Asia, sea farmers have been raising "crops" of fish like this for hundreds of years. Just as land farmers raise pigs and chickens.

But for fish farming in the distant future some oceanographers have dreamed up the most exciting idea of all. There are "dead" spots in the sea where currents don't stir up the water. Big fish usually don't live in these peculiar places.

The oceanographers want to run a giant pipe from the surface of these spots clear down to the ocean bottom. Once the pipe is filled with bottom water, so *they* say, water would keep running up!

These men believe that water gushing out of the pipe's top would make a current in the sea. Fish might move in and live here. Soon, the dead spots might turn into rich and fertile fishing spots.

Could this self-running fountain possibly work? You certainly would not think so. It sounds like a tale of pure science fiction.

But, in his laboratory at Woods Hole, Dr. Henry Stommel has built a small model of the fountain and tried it out.

It really works!

CHAPTER IX

Drifting pastures

In the deep blue sea live tiny plants that may be the world's most important food. They are called *diatoms* (*say: DIE-uh-toms*). These little plants wear glistening, glass-like shells. When you see a few diatoms under a microscope, their shells look like clear, sparkling boxes.

All the fierce fish depend on these fairylike plants— and a few other plants you can't see without a microscope. Here is why they are so important:

A thousand million BILLION little plants are clustered together in great sea pastures. As they drift back and forth in the waves, they are busy making food from chemicals that slosh around in the water. Tiny little animals—baby shrimp, baby octopuses, and copepods—"graze" hungrily in the brownish-green pastures.

Along come schools of little fish—herring, for example —and gobble up these grazers. Then big fish gulp down the little fish. No matter how big the gulping fish get, the whole chain of feeding begins with the little food plants.

These drifting plants, and the grazing animals that drift with them, make up the ocean's plankton. Some of the whales, the biggest creatures in the sea, feed on these tiny specks of life.

Sailors have told of watching the thrashing beasts charge back and forth through acres and acres of plankton. Water gushes from the sides of their mouths as they strain out and gulp down hordes of the organisms.

Some day you may eat plankton, too, if the world runs short of food. Perhaps you remember the story of how Thor Heyerdahl drifted across the Pacific on a raft. He caught some plankton with a fine, delicate net and boiled them in a soup. They made a tasty meal.

There is another kind of plant, very different from a diatom, which drifts over miles and miles of sea. It is called *Sargassum* (*say: Sar-GAS-sum*), the most famous seaweed in the world. Clumps of this plant float in the middle of the deep Atlantic. They float where Columbus found them nearly five hundred years ago.

As far as Columbus could see, great gobs of the yellow-brown plant lay drifting. His three little ships took two weeks to plow through all the stringy clumps.

Most sea plants have root-like parts that hold them

to rocks in shallow water. But Sargassum floats in water three miles deep! How? Little sacs of air that look like grapes grow out from the stems. They hold the seaweed up.

The miles and miles of water covered by the weed is named the *Sargasso* Sea (*say: Sar-GAS-so*). This sea is about as big as the whole great continent of Europe. Today about ten million tons of Sargassum float in the Sea.

60

The Sargasso Sea is a quiet place, unruffled by winds and waves. But to the west, the great Gulf Stream rushes by. The Stream flows up from the South, and curls northeast around the great mass of plants. Its force, rushing by the edge of the plants, keeps the whole heavy mass turning lazily around.

There are seas of Sargassum in the Pacific and Antarctic oceans. But the great island floating in the Atlantic is the most famous of the three. For centuries the Sargasso Sea has been shrouded in fear and mystery.

Early sailors told of seeing the dark, ghostly hulks of ships caught among the plants. Sea captains steered around the sea for fear of getting stuck in its center. But the old tales are not true. *You* could row a boat through the sea and not get caught in the weed.

How did the Sargasso Sea begin? No one knows. But the first Sargassum probably ripped away from the seacoasts and drifted into the middle of the ocean. And there the weed began to grow.

Little coastal creatures went along for the ride. Some of them turned yellow-brown to match the color of the seaweed. Today, if you could sneak up close to a clump of Sargassum, you would see a strange little world. It could happen only in the Sargasso Sea:

A funny little crab hiding under a leaf. A flying fish building a nest of leaves for its eggs. A tiny seahorse

standing on its tail curled around a stem. A flabby snail creeping along without a shell. A water strider, like a spider, dancing across the water—on six long hairy legs.

Sargassum weed probably does nothing more useful than make a home for these busy creatures. But a substance taken from kelp, a close cousin of Sargassum, helps man in many ways. It is used in making ice cream!

And cake icing, jelly, and candy. The kelp substance is also put into medicine, salad dressing, rubber, paint, glue, cloth, and paper. Kelp itself is ground up for fertilizer.

Most of our kelp grows in great clusters in the sunny waters off the West Coast. It is a tough brown plant with straight stalks that may grow a hundred feet high.

Sea creatures live in a forest of kelp as land animals live in a dense jungle. Even swift tuna find shelter there. For skin divers who hunt fish with a spear, a kelp bed is a paradise.

For oceanographers who hunt facts with instruments, the whole great ocean is a paradise. Let's see how these scientists hunt, and what sort of facts they "catch."

CHAPTER X

A seahunt for facts

Have you ever stood high on a mountaintop and shouted across a valley? If you have, you know that the echo of your voice bounces back to you. Echoes of sound bounce back from the ocean floor in the same sort of way.

Sound can travel through water as quick as a wink. It tells oceanographers how deep the sea is. An echo sounder on a ship sends "pings" of sound down to the ocean floor. Then it measures how long the pings take to bounce back.

When a ship sails over the surface, it can send out

pings which are as steady as the ticks of a clock. Echoes, short and long, come back steadily to the ship. The scientists can make a good record of the rise and fall of the ocean floor.

Making this record, or map, of the bottom was not always so easy. Scientists did it the hard way some ninety years ago. Oceanography then was just getting started.

In 1872 some British scientists began an explorer's voyage aboard the *H. M. S. Challenger*. For more than three years they hunted the sea for new facts. When the men wanted to measure the ocean's depth, they tied a weight to a long rope and flung it over the ship's side.

When the weight touched bottom, the men measured the length of rope that had been pulled into the water. Then they could tell the depth at that spot. The deepest spot these scientists found was almost five miles down. Imagine standing on a deck and unwinding this much rope! It took the men hours and hours.

The *Challenger* scientists could make only a rough map of the ocean basins. The basins have three main parts: the continental shelf, the continental slope, and the abyss. When you wade into the water from a beach, you are stepping on the shelf. This ledge makes a shallow border all around our continents.

Continental shelf　　Continental slope　　Abyss

Trench

The shelf slopes away gently from dry land. But, in about six hundred feet of water, the sea floor changes quickly into the steep continental slope. The slope drops down, down, down—to the broad plains of the abyss. Here the sea is a dark and gloomy place where few men have cared to go.

For many years, the basins were thought to be as smooth as a bathtub. As far as anyone knew, there were no exciting features like the mountains, valleys, cliffs, and canyons that are found on land.

But the invention of the echo sounder in the 1920's changed this idea of bareness. For the first time oceanographers could sail over big areas of water and make bottom maps filled with details. They could measure a depth in seconds instead of hours.

The scientists found strange canyons cut through the continental shelf and slope. They found long, deep cracks that slashed across the abyss. They learned that the ocean is full of jagged mountains—giant seamounts which rise up from the plains of the abyss.

Even now, there must be many unknown seamounts hidden underwater. Dr. Roger Revelle, a famous oceanographer, has said that we have good maps of only two per cent of the whole ocean floor!

In 1957 and 1958 oceanographers made an extra effort to map the unknown parts of the bottom of the sea. In the abyss of the Pacific, they found a deep crack —the Peru-Chile Trench. These men were taking part in the **IGY,** the International *Geophysical* Year (*say: jee-oh-FIZ-i-kl*). Sixty ships from forty countries set out to learn about the sea.

The scientists did much more than make maps of the ocean floor. Men on the ships dangled special cameras from long cables and made pictures of the sea floor. They took temperatures of the ocean, from the top right down to the bottom. And brought up hundreds of bottles filled with water—to be studied back on land.

At about the same time, two of our own nuclear submarines probed under the ice that covers the Arctic Ocean. One sub, the *Triton*, followed Magellan's path clear around the world—under water!

In the middle of the Atlantic, the *Triton's* echo sounder picked out an unknown seamount nine thousand feet high. And then the sounder broke down. Until the crew repaired it, the sub was in great danger. It could have crashed blindly into another unknown mountain!

Now you can see why it is so important to make maps of the rugged ocean floor. Today our nuclear submarines help to guard our country. Men on the subs must know what sea dangers they are likely to meet.

Some oceanographers are not content to let the echo sounder make map-pictures of the bottom. They want to *see* what big bottom areas look like. As you read this page, scientists may be cruising over the ocean floor in a new and special submarine. The little sub, named the *Aluminaut* (*say: uh-LOOM-i-not*), can carry three men. It can dive fifteen thousand feet down into the sea and prowl around for many hours.

What will the scientists find down there? New clumps of minerals? Old clumps of mud? Cliffs and cracks and seamounts? Strange fish that have been hiding for centuries?

The scientists won't know until they look. In fact, they have a great deal of looking to do through all of the

ocean world. Oceanographers of the National Academy of Sciences have made plans for ten years of seahunting.

The Navy and the National Science Foundation are going to spend millions of dollars on the plans. Already some sleek new ships are being built. By 1970 we can hope to see eighty-five ships of science working on the high seas.

The oceanographers hope, too, that young people will follow in their footsteps. They think that good students should get scholarships to study the sea. Perhaps *you* will want to make the ocean your life's work.

Our future on land may depend on just how much you—and other scientists of tomorrow—learn about the deep blue sea!

INDEX

Abyss, 33, 67, 68
Aegean Sea, 43
Africa, 13, 16, 20, 31
Aluminaut, 69
Anderson, Dr. Victor, 36
Antarctic Ocean, 17, 61
Aqualung, 25, 28, 42
Arctic Ocean, 17, 68
Atlantic Ocean, 15, 17, 29, 46, 54, 60, 61, 68

Bahamas, 26
Barton, Otis, 29, 31
Bascom, Willard, 38, 39
Bathyscaph, 31, 33, 36
Bathysphere, 29, 30, 31
Beast, The, 36, 38
Beebe, Dr. William, 29, 30, 31
Bony fish, 34
Bottle, 7, 8, 9, 68
Bronze, 44
Bumpus, Dean F., 9

Caesarea, 41, 42
California, 35, 46
Camera, 68
Canada, 51
Caribbean, 44
Caspian Sea, 54
Challenger, H. M. S., 65
Cliff, 67, 69
Coast Guard, 8
Coelacanth, 21, 22
Columbus, 15, 60
Continental shelf, 65, 67
Continental slope, 65, 67
Copepod, 58
Copper, 43, 44, 46
Coral, 25, 26; coral reef, 25, 44
Coring tube, 38
Courtenay-Latimer, Miss M., 20
Cousteau, Capt. Jacques-Ives, 22, 23, 24, 25, 28

Crab, 62
Current, 8, 9, 10, 55, 56

Diatom, 57, 60
Dinosaur, 21
Diver, 24, 25, 26, 27, 28, 42, 43, 44

Earthquake, 37, 42
Echo sounder, 64, 67, 68, 69
Egg, 9, 62
Europe, 54, 60

Florida Keys, 44
Flounder, 34
Flying fish, 62
Food, 10, 57, 58, 59
Fossil, 21, 22
Fundy, Bay of, 51

Gagnan, Emile, 25
Glacier, 37
Gulf Stream, 9, 61

Haddock, 9
Herring, 53, 55, 58
Heyerdahl, Thor, 59

Ichthyologist, 20
Indian Ocean, 16, 17, 20, 46
International Geophysical Year, 68

Kelp, 62, 63

La Jolla, California, 35, 36
Light organ, 33, 34
Limestone, 26
Link, Edwin, 42
Lisbon, Portugal, 12, 15

Magellan, Ferdinand, 13, 15, 16, 17, 68
Magnesium, 46
Maine, 53; Gulf of, 9
Manfish, 22, 25, 27, 28

Manganese, 44
Mediterranean, 19, 23, 25, 41, 42
Mero, Dr. John, 46
Mexico, Gulf of, 46
Minerals, 44, 46, 49
Monster, 13, 15, 16, 17, 35, 36
Moray eel, 28
Mountain, 11, 12, 31, 67, 68
Mud, 36, 37, 38, 42, 69

National Academy of Sciences, 40, 70
National Science Foundation, 40, 70
New Zealand, 54
Nickel, 46
Nile River, 19
Nodule, 46
North Sea, 54
Nova Scotia, 51

Oceanographer, 8, 9, 17, 25, 36, 44, 55,
    63, 64, 67, 68, 69, 70
Oceanography, 65
Octopus, 58
Oil, 44, 46, 49
Oxygen, 10

Pacific Ocean, 15, 17, 31, 35, 46, 54, 59,
    61, 68
Palestine, 42
Pearl, 24
Piccard, Auguste, 31
Piccard, Jacques, 31, 34
Pipe, 38, 55, 56
Philippine Islands, 15
Plankton, 54, 58, 59
Pressure, 30, 34
Project Mohole, 40

Radioactive waste, 10
Red Sea, 19
Reef, 25, 26, 28, 43, 44
Revelle, Dr. Roger, 67
Rock, 24, 28, 36, 37, 40

Salmon, 52; Chinook, 54
Sargasso Sea, 60, 61, 62
Scripps Institute of Oceanography, 36
Seahorse, 62

Seamount, 67, 68, 69
Seaport, 12, 15
Seaweed, 60, 62
Sediment, 37, 38, 40
Shad, 52
Shell, 24, 37, 62
Shark, 20, 26, 27, 28
Shrimp, 30, 58
Silt, 37
Skin diver, 24, 25, 63
Smith, Dr. J. L. B., 20, 21
Snail, 62
Soft clam, 54
South America, 15
Spain, 15, 16, 44
Sponge, 24
Squid, 19, 30
Stommel, Dr. Henry, 56
Striped bass, 54
Submarine, 68, 69

Temperature, 68
Texas, 49
Throckmorton, Peter, 43
Tide, 9, 52
Treasure, 11, 24, 40, 42, 44, 46, 49
Trench, 31; Peru-Chile, 68
Triton, 68
Tuna, 55, 63

Undercurrent, 9
United States, 53
United States Fish and Wildlife Serv-
    ice, 9
Uranium, 44

Valley, 64, 67
Victoria, 16
Volcano, 37

Walsh, Lieut. Don, 31, 34
West Coast, 63
Whale, 58; Killer, 55
Wind, 37, 42, 61
Woods Hole Oceanographic Institution,
    8
Woods Hole, 9, 56
World Ocean, The, 17